Sizes

Contents

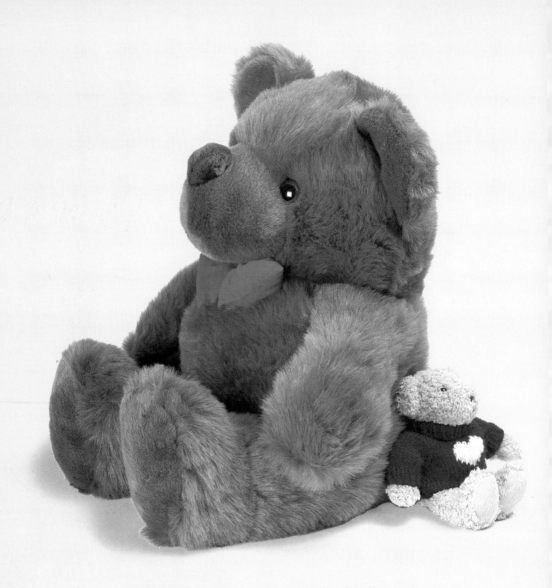

Which is bigger?

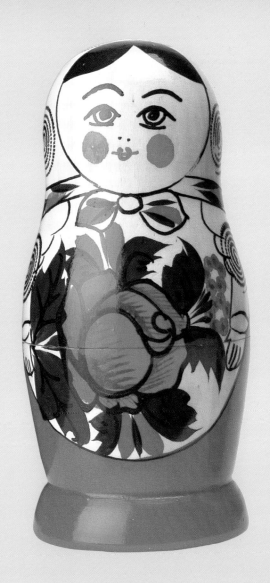
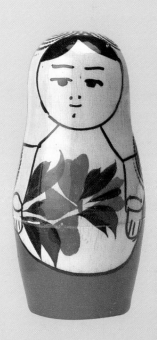

Which is smaller?

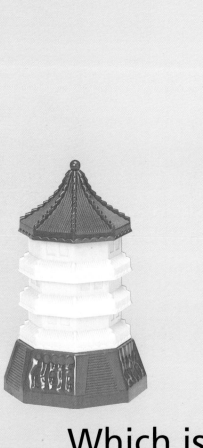
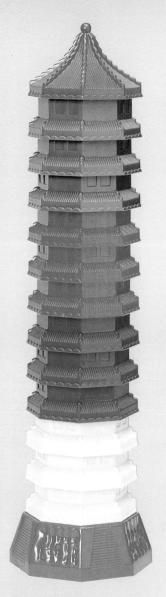

Which is taller?

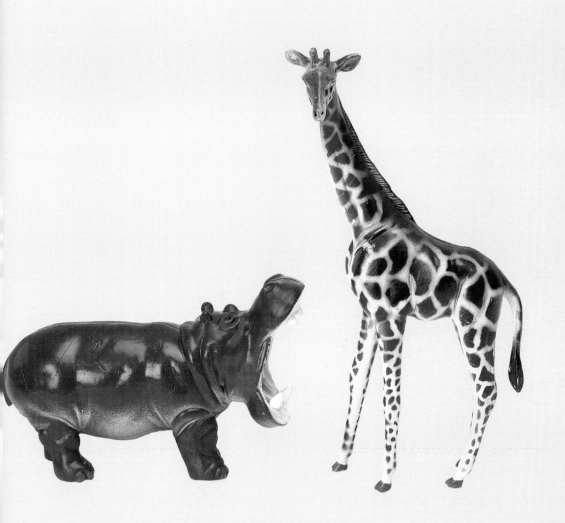

Which is shorter?

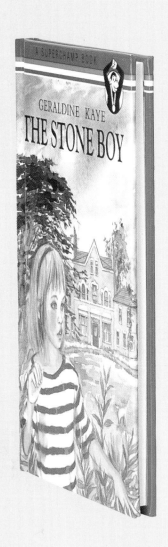

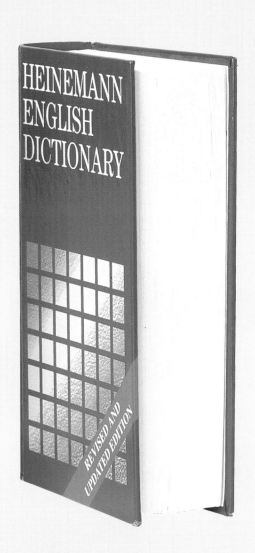

Which is thicker?

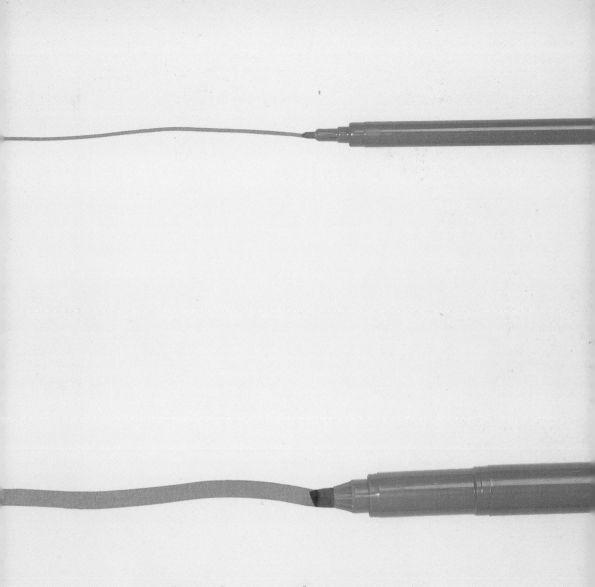

Which is thinner?

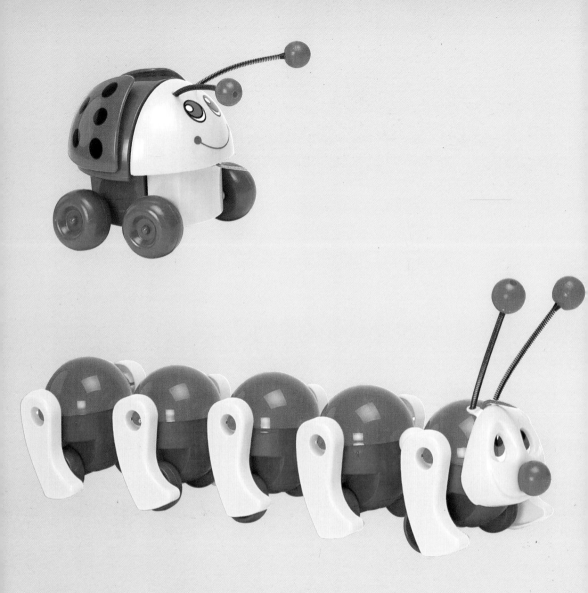

Which is longer?

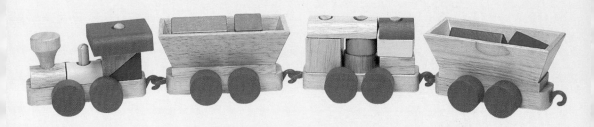

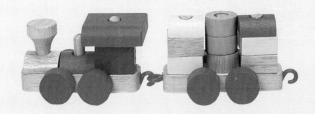

Which is shorter?

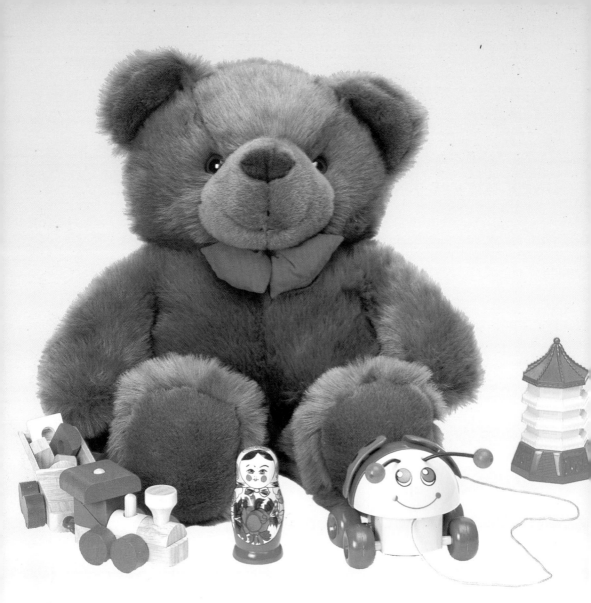

Which is the biggest?

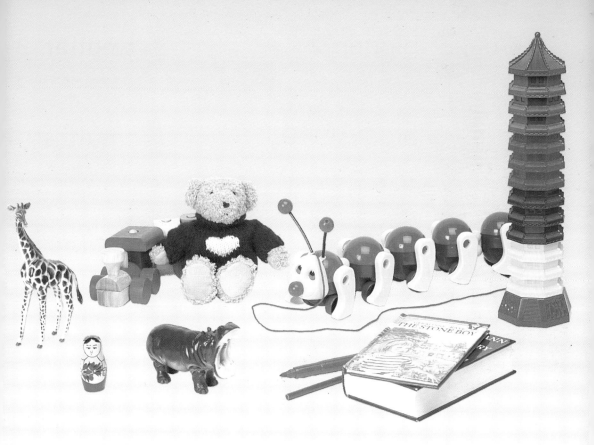

Which is the smallest?

Index and Answers

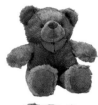

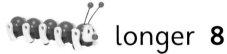

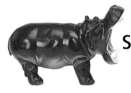

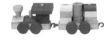